Reading Novalis in Montana

Reading Novalis in Montana

Melissa Kwasny

milkweed
editions

Milkweed Editions
1011 Washington Avenue South
Suite 300
Minneapolis, Minnesota 55415.
(800) 520-6455
www.milkweed.org

Published 2009 by Milkweed Editions

Printed in the United States of America

Cover design by Jeenee Lee

Cover art, "The Miracle of the Pitanga Tree," by Erica Harris

Author photo by Joseph Collins

Interior design by Paul Hotvedt

The text of this book is set in Warnock Pro.

13   14   15   16   17   5   4   3   2

First Edition

Library of Congress Cataloging-in-Publication Data

Kwasny, Melissa, 1954-
    Reading Novalis in Montana /
Melissa Kwasny. — 1st ed.
        p.   cm.
    ISBN 978-1-57131-429-1 (pbk. with flaps : acid-free paper)
    I. Title.
PS3561.W447R43 2009
    811´.54—dc22   2008017064

This book is printed on acid-free paper.

Please turn to the back of this book for a list of the sustaining funders of Milkweed Editions.

Contents

Acknowledgments

Grateful acknowledgment is made to the editors of the following publications in which some of these poems first appeared:

Bellingham Review: "Sleep Comes from the Flowers," "The Waterfall" (sections I-VII), "Soul," and "Earth" (from "The Directions")
Columbia: A Journal of Literature and Art: "The Ice-Lit Upper World" and "Orpheus"
Cutthroat: A Journal of the Arts: "The Under World"
Drumlummon Views: "The Waterfall" (sections VIII–XII)
Many Mountains Moving: "Beauty" and "Mule Deer"
Poetry Northwest: "Redpolls" and "Lepidoptera"
Ploughshares: "Common Blue"
Quarterly West: "Bee Balm"
River Styx: "Pond Ice"
Seneca Review: "Demeter"
South Dakota Review: "Brook Trout"
The Threepenny Review: "River Reeds" and "Reading a Biography of Ezra Pound in the Garden"
Willow Springs: "Black Geese in the Honey-Stubble of Fields Near Spring," "Reading Novalis in Montana," "My Heart Like an Upside-Down Flame," and "Sibyl"

"Reading Novalis in Montana" also appears in the anthology *Poems Across the Big Sky* (Lowell Jaeger, editor). "Reading Novalis in Montana," "Lepidoptera," and "Common Blue" also appear in the anthology *Montana Women Writers: A Geography of the Heart* (Carolyn Patterson, editor). "The

Under World" won the Joy Harjo Prize from *Cutthroat: A Journal of the Arts.*

I would like to acknowledge the authors of the following italicized lines: Robert Browning in "Calpyso," Ezra Pound in section 9 of "The Waterfall" (translated from the Latin: Tempus est ubique/ non motus/ in vesperibus orbis), and Plato in "Debt." In the long sequence "The Directions," the italicized lines in the section "Light" are taken from the titles of paintings by Morris Graves.

I want also to thank the following fine friends and wise readers of this manuscript: Patricia Goedicke, Robert Baker, and Rusty Morrison.

Reading Novalis in Montana

I

The incomplete still appears the most bearable.
Novalis

Reading Novalis in Montana

The dirt road is frozen. I hear the geese first in my lungs.
    Faint hieroglyphic against the gray sky.

Then, the brutal intervention of sound.
    All that we experience is a message, he wrote.

I would like to know what it means
    if first one bird swims the channel

across the classic *V,* the line flutters, and the formation dissolves.
    In the end, the modernists must have meant,

it is the *human* world we are weary of,
    our arms heavy with love, its ancient failings.

But that was before the world wars, in 1800,
    when a young German poet could pick at the truth

and collect the fragments in an encyclopedia of knowledge.
    There is a *V,* then an *L,* each letter

forming so slowly that the next appears before it is complete.
    The true philosophical act is the slaying of one's self,

Novalis wrote, and died, like Keats, before he was thirty.
    They have left me behind like one of their lost,

scratching at the gravel in the fields. Where are they
    once the sky has enveloped them?

I stand in the narrow cut of a frozen road leading into mountains,
    the morning newspaper gripped under my arm.

But to give up on things precludes everything.
    I am not-I, Novalis wrote. *I am you.*

If, as the gnostics say, the world was a mistake
        created by an evil demiurge, and I am trapped

in my body, abandoned by a god whom I long for as one of my own,
        why not follow the tundra geese into their storm?

Why stay while my great sails flap the ice
        as if my voice were needed to call them back

in the spring, as if I were the lost dwelling place for the flocks?

Redpolls

For days they have swarmed the thistle bag
like flies to a sweet.
The snow began early and broadened.
They lifted in two flocks from the side of the alder,
circled the slough of willows
as if they would be coming back, then further out,
toward the circumference, and they were gone.
I was there when the hundred redpolls decided
to leave my life, scarlet tag
on their foreheads, pink wash on their breasts.
Tundra birds, the book says. Circumpolar.
The winds now are distant. I dare not look up,
my feet filthy with ash and the too-early night,
my backseat with food wrappers, bags of laundry.
No wonder I want to buy something new:
red hair, or a lipstick in a shade called poppy,
an orchid strap that peeks from under my clothes.
The way I like to hear myself talk when
I've had wine and am well read, the way I don't
believe in mountain lions unless I've seen them—
this winter, the light never touching the walls,
what is it that I was supposed to learn?
Day drizzles through, marsh-pit and alabaster.
The slur, that's what I can't stand, from moment
to moment, yet, this morning, I saw the redpolls
leave for good. An irruptive species,
the books says, which means they won't be back
next year or next, like my grandmother, for instance.
So, after work, I make popcorn, fill her green bowl,
take it out to the creek where she might find it.
I love it here, too, though the great things I want—
to speak with the dead, to unfurl my nerves
in some kind of exhaustive wind,
to become disciplined and productive—elude me.
I read of Artaud who was tortured by his own mind,
how he felt his own mind wasn't his.

We all seem to live in approximation to our lives,
surrounded by a bevy of ghosts who,
stripped of their voices, mime and wave us to some
seat of origin. A swarm, a foreign country,
they approach and fade and finally, I think,
they give up on us. Not like the chickadees
who will come to my hand,
who blacken the snow beneath them with husks.

Mountains

Everyone is gone now but me and the mule deer
who are soft gray and separating into gender.
At three, cold begins to enter the rooms.
Finch nest, flicker, damask on leaves of willow.

They are right above my head, above the narrow
swath of my present. I catch their movement.
How is it they make no sound?
I live at the mountains' feet, a scrap, an offering.

The fir logs are lavender and easy to split, nothing
like the difficult gnarly pine. Frozen, by now,
the lips of the creek. The mountains live deep.
Their path is through water. What do they store

in those closets of pine, the mahogany glower
of their slopes? Is it inner power we seek
or a communion? Of course, there is always
the blessing of companionship, but the question:

Have we not lost our silver? I, for one, will
remember this place, how sun breaks through clouds
and the pulse expands. I often speak
of reading the world: its prints, its stones, its water.

I split wood to last the month, stack the larder
with wet aspen, which smells dirty when it burns—
blackened herbs, the dust of mountains.
I am too busy to be happy, studded with the snow.

Mule Deer

The same small herd in the woody slump of the creek bottom
down from the mountain, the arterial paths
in procession like pilgrims toward their vespers
       to iris bulbs warmed on the edge-wood of the garden
       to the water, simple
       to the clematis, long gone
I splash sunflower seeds out of a bucket onto the snow
The doe is pregnant and hay would make her bloat
She is the color of stoneware, sleep-filled
When the emerald returns in June they'll climb out of here to meet it
For now, the snow is marked with their split hearts
Cartographers, queens of trespass, they draw their blue lines
       best incline down, the shortest distance to raspberry
See how they mince like the herons do
But to be dazzled by the image is to be stuck there
Birds draw lines in air, fish in water, and the element closes up
       behind them—not earth, its endless embassies of departure
Sometimes I walk the deer paths which never stop or start
I know they lead from dream to water
The mule deer climb their stairwells under spruce toward the stars
       and here is where their absence will replace them

Pond Ice

Yesterday, the girl and I disturbed its sleep with rocks.
                The circumference groaned and splintered.
We made our way toward the center
which was open and swift, water graphite, sand at the bottom hazel.
We picked and sank the dark day there
through a forest resistant to our steps, through marsh clump,
                      ice crust, the long-needled ground.
Tiny birdlike finger bones pressed into the snow—
                    field mice hurrying to the next log.
Alyce was suspicious. She traced our tracks with a stick
            though I told her I have been this way a hundred times.
Love is hard, and I feel so old this winter. The roots of my coarse hair
            grow pale. I bury my voice
in the plum banks of my moon clots, drench my nights in chardonnay.
Last night, I caught her whimpering in her makeshift bed,
            afraid that her mother won't come back for her.
She shredded tissues into rags,
stained them resin and ochre, while my heart leaked its slow, dirty tears.
Need is embarrassing, something that seeps.
            We both believe it to be our thrift if we do not.
This morning, while she was sleeping, I read about the surrealists,
            their goal to infuse reality with the divine.
                      Thought comes syntactically.
André Breton is amazed. Yet, saying that, he must know that it comes
doggedly. Breakthrough is such a human wish,
            the surface pitted with the asterisks of our failed attempts.
And so, we stand here again today, the water
knocking, bleeding black as it passes under and sometimes through the ice.

Brook Trout

Six rubies in a row on its golden flank, more distinctive
than the smallness of its name.
I teach her *brook trout* quick before its life sighs out of it
though it dries while I pull at the hook. I teach her
red-winged blackbird who nests in the cattails
that look instead like drumsticks she's seen her family
use at powwows. She asks: Why don't I have an Indian name?
She wants to pan for gold in a place I know
to be much the same as here: dark pines, a creek too small
to swim in. Yet, *Grizzly Gulch*, she pleads, her own Golconda.
We watch the tiniest fish run for the last scrap
of worm, then frighten and disappear under the bracken.
I teach her *lilac* because we planted it, *black-oil*
sunflower, wonder what would be her name if she could choose it.
Her grandfather once told me the Cree story of Wa-sak-a-chak,
first man, like Adam, so he got to name things.
Who came first, the fish or the stars? The stars, I tell her,
though by now I am a bit confused. Are we talking of
her tradition or of mine? I think it's a *miracle*, she says,
to try out that new word. She says *maryjesusgod,*
and now we're both confused. Lucky, another brook trout
comes spinning above the stream.
I say: A woman is not named rose because she likes them.

Black Geese in the Honey-Stubble of Fields Near Spring

Patchy with molt and milk, the sour smell of goose under the wing,
it is the bigness of the thing, how two squawk and break into it
as a car crunches past, how two more who are tied to them are pulled aloft.
There are more than a thousand. Their black necks sop
and crane down the large valley between the Bitterroots and the Skalkaho,
the milder, older ridges to the right. Me in my red
anorak against the spring light, which is brazen and begs to be taken back.
Your pain—how could I have said it—is out of all proportion.
You remember from your years by this river that some rocks will have rings.
I follow miserly, afraid to take anything. Mauve, chalk-gray,
you build your pastel pile while the geese write marginalia above us.
Winter, and the river is seamless, not polyglot. We walk
until it crosses our path. This is before the balance is upset again.
When we are faithful to each other and true. I watch what you select
because I could never choose for you who collect and discard so prolifically.
Look, I was never much for family. Yet here we are.
The willow stems are turning, the dogwood almost blue, the stones
you bring back are stone and plum. You show me
where the beavers have chiseled the white pulp of the trunk
into the shape of an hourglass until it falls. Why don't you cut with me here
across the fields far from the river, through the crush
of mown peppermint and crust of hay. Let us scatter these geese,
watch them circle north, or south. It is uncertain just how virtuous they are.

My Heart Like an Upside-Down Flame

title from a poem by Guillaume Apollinaire

One walks, or wants to walk, with the glow
cupped by two hands. As if light were water.

As if lemon verbena,
a blossom around the solid figure of the wick.

But look what can happen.
The heart has been looted of its small valuables:

music, of course, and the dancing couple
from childhood, secure in their velvet-lined box.

What is it that so captivates us in the old cliché?
I am thinking of the light cast from the pines

or the first green shoots of onion.
Bird in the palm if only we were patient enough.

We who lay the fragile thing beating in the yard,
then trust the stray cat won't find it.

Here is the pile of gray feathers and grit.
Who was it who told us courage was a virtue?

A candle burns at solstice on a simple yellow plate.
After work hours, after the bills are paid.

The safe heart then, burrowed into its winter cave?
Fish bones and behind them, swimming.

What is it that I expected the heart to do?
Follow me? A handmaid, arranging the bouquets?

Or this tree, then that one, a row of grayer birch
as the flame steps out from the shadows of its house.

Is It Oblivion or Absorption When Things Pass from Our Minds?

title from a line in a letter by Emily Dickinson

The bedroom winds that swept in from the south last night
have flattened into something curious and deep

though there is yellow sun left in the bald patches of yard,
wainscoting of sun on the shingles, and a new blowzy chorus

of winds has begun somewhere in the mountains above me.
The house shifts. The plastic over the woodpile swells, resists.

Sunlight drapes the broad shoulders of the canyon, flickers
over the dark fist at its heart. I must climb out if I am to find it.

I will be caught in the vegetable dark. Here, where the self stalls
in the hiss between channels, in the sound of gravel shoveled,

the sound of excavation. Earth teeth, yet who can speak for anyone?
I hide in my house, deaf to the gods of this hour, their tackle

and toll bridge, and eke along, crossing the day on crutches,
crossing the cement-blue square of each day, each with a sky

that sucks the clouds into it, quick crowding of blue to the drain.
My mind: I want to stand up to it. Is there such a thing as irretrievable

intelligence? Give me one small task, one I can be happy with,
my hands meeting the same hand-like muscle of the dough,

but still, the need to rush on, to prove something.
There is too much to read for me to feel well-read, the collective

push against the portal of the father, the mother, or the sister
who drinks too much wine. It can break your heart, these lists

we keep that keep going under, the handwritten
need so clearly spelled out: peanut butter, milk, always coffee.

The throwaway life? Always, it seems, we'd trade disposability
for a room where time swells like white beans and thyme, flavors

the wide body of the soup. Where do they pass to, *our subjects*?
Like seeds that land in the crook of a willow branch, do they tumble

down later into the loam? Or drop like an earring between the slats
of the porch floor, a gleam we can see but can't reach?

Common Blue

Their eggs are laid on lupine. Tiny green
hairstreaks I could easily mistake for dew.
Too precious. Too incidental,
these trills that flounce in my potato patch,
drawn from dryland origins to the domestic
stain of water from my hose.
What an old woman would study, I think
as you hand me the guidebook, distracted
by the replica of a parasol
growing out of a bleached cow pie.
The Siamese kitten with his butterfly eyes
comes running, his mouth full
of swallowtail, his breath smelling of borax
and sugar I have poured
over the anthills in the garden.
He is young and intent on eating poison.
We bushwhack through paradise—
what is there to say except to lament
the daily evidence of its passing,
how the Common Blues scatter from my shade.
And you, so fragile, so sick, so thin,
your diet restricted, keep pointing out
the bearded face of larkspur.
When the angels fell, a fifteenth-century bishop says,
there were 133,306,668 of them.
It takes us all afternoon to cross the field.
The body, it is so sad what happens to it.
If you fell, you would dry up instantly.
But these are not Angelwings
who disguise themselves as leaf or shred of bark,
who are named after the stops
in meaning our language must make room for:
the Comma whose wings look battered,
or the violet underside of the Question Mark.
To keep the mind from clenching, you say,
is the main thing. Even the most

beautiful days always seem to have death in them.
As Valentinus says: our fall into love and sleep.
You especially like the dark Alpines
with their furred bodies and lack of marking.
And the Sulphurs, yellowed scraps that fall
from a myth of origin that doesn't include us.
When we find them, we will wonder
who is still alive. We speak of our souls with such
surface ease. But who will take such care for us?
You bend and bend to the scrappy blue sea,
your back turned to the moon fluttering above you.
I have been thinking so much of strength
this week, yours and mine, I mean,
the field of attention that can be strengthened.

Lepidoptera

more brilliancy, starriness, quain, margaretting!
GERARD MANLEY HOPKINS

The Wood Nymph steadies itself on a grass blade
with one of its six legs. It landed clumsily.
It has been mating in air. Common Sulphur
on the sunflower. Cabbage White on the yarrow.
Black trim of the Pine White caught in a web.
Perhaps the argument begins here, when I am late,
when things are browning. A week ago,
all was gauze-green, billowing in the breezes.
One could hardly choose between velvet and cob.
There was coolness for thirst, the equivalent
of our gin and tonics. The bulbous spree of mullein,
yellow-tipped, made the pasture a candelabra.
And as the butterflies steered through this forest
of soft things and the eccentric, of towers, tridents,
the sun-warmed mint, the musk of thistle,
they would land and close their wings as if in prayer.
One reads the world the best one can,
bloom of bull thistle changing from fuchsia to purple,
the purple not a color but an event.
Even the berries are translucent.
This is how it must be for them, the vegetable world
standing between them and the sun, glimmer
through fir trees in the morning: priests, intermediaries,
interlocutors. Why do the female Wood Nymphs
have larger eyespots than the males do?
Why do Dark Wood Nymphs visit flowers more than others?
Would you trade your eighty years
for their two weeks of bliss, blue gentian, a chance
to mate in air? It takes years for some species—
egg to caterpillar, to pupa, gates of the chrysalis

to open wide—yet two years of the non-ecstatic
are life, too. And aren't there times
when they have felt, as we in turn have felt,
that gorged with such goodness they could die now?

Bee Balm

I know that no one would live out
Thirty years, fifty years if the world were ending
With his life.
GEORGE OPPEN

Swan necks and wings   mint petals in the heat by the water
Sun split   I can smell them   almost gardenia

Chime of the junkos soft in dead limbs
Oregon grape have stopped their flowering and turned blue

Blue phase of last flowering   the large headed bee balm
lift their shaggy heads   skull cap of the pistil fringed by curls

If taste were color, sugar would be this lavender   darling
to the bees   who live their half-season over the double-decked

Fritillary on the thistle   an orange flock   is this enough for us
we   who want to be recognized for our goodness too

No there is work to do   even now when we can be
what it is easy to be   nomadic between our skin and the world

One starts out simply   bee balm stands out against *plein air*
If we knew the world would end with our lives

We who have learned sunwise   to turn to the left
we who have learned origin within end   soon we won't be able

to eat or sleep outdoors   ground will freeze   these petals
fade and seed   a taste that cools the tongue   bitter-lasting

Beauty

Once I thought it was like this winter morning
through the window still with frost and the frozen
water no wind too cold for wind a zero balance an absolute
necessity though with tiny movements a little flux
and reflux as they say because the mind that gets stuck is
rarely beautiful we must have the chickadee
and nuthatch whirring back to the tree a kind of willow
thin of course as is its nature two limbs cracked off
in the last heavy snow so that the color is fresh not a scab
of gray bark but yellow pealing expository just two
the rest pink with frost like the downy hair on a woman's arm
held to the light what Eliot didn't like the unsmooth
unperfected why we get along so well you and I because
thought like love fades into something else so quickly
perhaps two dozen leaves which still hang at the tips
not their shape but absence of shape of color
how the small birds blend in the azure that expounds them
beauty doesn't fade does it betray confuse look how even
dead like this asleep the earth is bringing the tiny scales
of frost into existence if art is selection hence interpretation
in an ink drawing not everything is sketched in but what is
is given a place of honor today the birds
float latched to the tree to fly must be much like swimming

The Beautician

She wants to dye my hair some thirteen shades
of russet, brown, and leave some gray,
a mow of dam and cedar. She wants it
invested and waxy with beeswax and plum,
or like the lightning-split pine whose dead
limbs are lined with dark bird after bird—
of course, she will make it all look natural.
The tops of the fir trees are glutted now
with migrants. I assume I know the world news
because they come to my feeder,
because I can count their names on one hand.
She says: dye it a strawberry that brings in
the starving. You've been babysitting
far from the deep. A rope spirals down
and I pull up water which the ancients say
will strengthen my wings.
Inside the earth, it is cloudy, not clear.
She says: whoever feels most deeply wins.
Look, I exercise. Eat well. I work and pray.
Why am I so sorry in my tent for the night?
Come in, she says, where the sauce is marinara,
where they shred red peppers in your eggs.
She is crying so hard now, I think it is me,
a sloughing off of the uterine lining.
Me, as surface? Me, familiar? Me,
with no surprises left? I want to be central,
then all the way out to the brim of being.
Your hair will be faithless, she says,
an outcrop, sex spilling over into everything.

Visiting H.D.'s Grave in Bethlehem, Pennsylvania

White stone, and a sage-green bloom of mold
clings to the edges of her name.
The steel mill is silent below me, across the river.
Older graves darken from the corrosion of acid rain.
I purchase white violets,
blue violets in a hamlet on the way, roots
crammed into plastic pots where they were sown.

It is too early for hyacinths in eastern Pennsylvania.
The elm trees are leafless, the town threadbare,
bombed out, as if in a war. *The rain falls, here, there,*
she wrote, *the shrine lies open to the sky.*
She never saw this, what happened to the barns.

The poet, they say, lies here under my feet,
long limbs like roots now, disengaged from their leaves,
she who had once wanted to be named Tree.

Violets, not hyacinths. How can any of us stand
the scenes? There is *vision of the womb*, she wrote,
and vision of the brain. By then, she wasn't
thinking of her home in Pennsylvania, the foundries,
how the coal-shadows would press their thumbs down.
Even she knew that image was not enough.

Hay-bright next to the diurnal earth, by the green plaque,
below the Christian temple, her stone laid flat,
the old way, her ex-husband's name carved upon it.

I have seen her as Eurydice, pale in Greek gown.
I have seen her as a young troubadour
in the famous portrait by Man Ray, her bangs cut blunt,
her robe androgynous. Madame Sosostris
with her wicked pack of cards, what
is she doing here, away from all she had become?

Reading a Biography of Ezra Pound in the Garden

Wet, limp, as if just born, the five petals unstick
from each other. *I have blundered always,*
said Ezra Pound. The hot winds of Venice
blow past my bare ankles, a cat sprawls on its side
across the lawn. *I don't know how humanity stands it,*
the heat he might mean, too much going on
and much of it boring. He writes: *I am homesick
after mine own kind.* The zucchini, everyone
knows, is prolific. While my guests come and go,
pilfering my time, it offers one green fruit a day,
and these flowers like lap cloths unfolded.
Could it be that I have given another summer away,
intent on my own distractibility, the flowers
like tiles in a Cordovan kitchen or the American
orange color of margarine? The precision it requires
to translate the lyric, the Greek hexameter,
the ancient Chinese character—I am so used
to the open that, when I go inside, I leave
all the house doors ajar. Life, Pound told his daughter,
must always involve suffering. It exists
in order to make people think. Fact: the forest
begins at the end of my porch. Trees circle
the house like a choir. Oh, the west, it turns the green
orange-rose, allows the pines to stand and move
forward. The path I walk is dry and apparent now.
How can we not be human when it is this August wind
that prepares us, when we can't stomach
one more sweet grain? Look, how the spring-rocks
have grown a coat of lichen. Nature—he called it time—
winds its way into the alley-space. Season,
a word that means *to sow.* Pound knew that the days
would string together, that what isn't finished
today would have its bloom. Yet, *I cannot
make it cohere,* the poet wrote in his *Cantos,*
fruit coming so thick he couldn't possibly use it,
overfilling the tin bucket by the back door.

II

To have gathered from the air a
live tradition.
Ezra Pound

The Waterfall

1

The rags fade in their frame of overbent willow, prayer
        flags laid in a web of leaf-silver
Squat, the womb-hut stripped of its tarps and blankets
        is spooked and lifting from the lake

Whose voice is duck feet that drag in their own wake
        a drowsy soft wood with the peck
of the old ones in it who quicken to their language spoken
        a language that is stricken and is floral

Lichen, arrowroot, arnica, alder, the wild Calypso orchid
        with its spotted, cloven tongue
the maw-red wicks of the Rocky Mountain maple
        which candle into green, then tier

The days are paved in gold before them, have no fear
        that they will squander them
pondering their own matched angel of light whose voice
        is like a paintbrush treated too brusquely

With petals dipped in sun-bleach, celadon, dust-pink
        The thoughts of an heiress, tousled
and bed-mad, spring out in no order at whim and at wood
        A tree hangs with the blue ribbons of its own wind

In the painting by Franz Marc, which I saw in the museum as a child, there is a waterfall and there are birds in it. The birds are blue and yellow and pink, not the shades birds are when they flock. He called the last of his series "The Fate of the Animals." Dark blossoms of cat prints in the mud.

Winter is trampled under the summer waterfall. You can hear it at a distance, grappling under ice, but for now, there is the green word *june* and the passive blue ones. I loved those words when I was young. I read their thoughts, could turn invisible, and drew small flowers on my palms with ink. This was no place for children, I knew early. The birds were red and flew from mirrors in warning.

The way down is always through water. You can recognize the stepping stones in the current, each with a number, each with its own ritual order of splashes. Hair shreds from roots near the shore. Granite rolls on its dirty white flanks. The dark bears in mourning, dragging their tire-marked legs. Guardians of the secret everywhere. There! The spiritual antennae of the elk are in velvet. There! The tombstone that has come to my grave before me. I go hooded in black although it is merely a sweatshirt. I go to beg for incantation:

> *I sing this song about myself, full sad.*
> I sing of disappearing things. Too bad—
> the dusky sparrow, snow geese wings
> tattooed with stripes, plover rings,
> blue fields of flax, bobcats that pounce,
> real saffron for six bucks an ounce,
> the native tribes in Deer Lodge jailed
> for writing checks that bounce, our failed
> intentions, Superfunds submerged in mire,
> the slick Ohio river caught on fire.

At the ninth level there are star-flowers, arrow-leaf sown across the field of closed vision. The descent is clumsy and dangerous in springtime, the frozen still in me, a hollow sound that cries out in warning like the great holy stones. The water-birds flashing in the trees. They say the old ones respond to the old ways and are drawn back. I give them canned salmon, berries, a smoke.

Visionary City! It shouldn't be so easy to get there, but it is. You can ask the dead for anything but life: money, safe travel, good gossip. Refugees, they have their blankets spread at all our art fairs.

3

I isolate them from each other by voice
and arrange them in family scenes: the argument,
neglect, the passionate declaration.
Here, for instance, a splash. She is the violet
rim of white, an intoxicated woman who fears
that once she starts, she won't stop laughing.
He is the motor. The larger fall is contained in him.
Gold-bronze, a soldier-god struck to the ground,
still suffering from the violence of his early marriage.
This is what calls to me just as I turn from it—
male, female, sometimes the voice of children.
Perhaps two boys, drowned last week in the reservoir.
Stepfather grieves. Mother is in jail for larceny.
The bodies of the boys are badly beaten.
Felt but not seen, over the shoulder, off the rocks—
but knowing who the voice belongs to has never helped.
The Greeks, of course, had a name for the spirits
in the waterfall, calling them Naiads or water nymphs.
The spirits were personified, but that is different,
as Rimbaud said, from recapturing voices of the dead.
In Montana, at the end of a dusty August logging road,
shallow with fool's gold and silt, the creek contains
the voice of a single woman singing, whose solitude,
the stories tell us, is cause for trouble. Keats
overhead it as Arethusa and Alpheus in the midst of
their sexual battle. Often, the threat of rape in myth.
Understandable, our reluctance to believe the songs.
Not quite a hundred years ago, in the hills
outside a western town named Helena, a band of Cree
were camped. While the men prayed and fasted
over the ridge, the women waited with their children
by the water. The cavalry came and massacred them.
But there is a part of the story I have only recently
learned, that when the women saw the soldiers coming,
their spirits fled into these rocks.
Today, potatoes and squash break the horizon of our soil.
Who believes enough to have a vision now?

4

Things do not happen in a line, but all at once, the choreographer says.

Choice then becomes arbitrary, as in the method of dance called contact improvisation.

You respond to whomever gets closest to you, presses her hand into your back.

Not spiritual, not channeling, she said. The response must come from inside your body.

All new projects then seem overwhelming, clouds and smoke.

The art of the unnecessary.

You remember your mother putting your crib outside and how the robins sang in and out of you.

In the mountains, there you feel free.

You either believe life is random or, like your mother says, that everything happens for a reason,

which would demand extraordinary vigilance from a god and a wider lens than you have.

Like the medicine man dreaming in the hospital that night, the night he almost died.

A tunnel of light, a guide who met him, his ancestors all so happy.

But why were they sitting on wagons and horses, not working, not doing anything?

"They are telling stories," his guide explained. "They are waiting for the new ones, to catch up."

If there is only one other side, vaster than this, is everything that isn't this the other side?

Those are not your relatives camped by the river, the ones with the blue lights.

Heraclitus said that fire passes by combustion into water and earth.

The reverse process occurs simultaneously when earth liquefies, evaporates, exhales into fire,

constituting a way up and a way down, a two-way process of interchange between the elements.

Something is always trying and failing to reach us.

Dark water and dark sky, the only difference in texture, the fluid more wrinkled.

Overhanging branches and perhaps a star.

5

When I am alone, I am godly.
>I have my small tasks which no one sees.
I dig the bull thistle furiously,
>the shovel slicing their white necks.
I pull the toadflax, a noxious weed
>that keeps coming back, water the wild
columbine with a bucket I keep by the stream.

I like to choose without anxiety,
>drop my tasks as easily as I let feathers
or the blue and white crumbs of eggshell slip.
>So, who is this self that everyone seeks?

The dead ones fit in the spaces between the spruces,
>faces, hollow-cheeked and hollow-eyed.
I know what you will say, what has been said
>before you: white people who want to play Indian.

Yet when the old Cree man prayed in front of me,
>I kept my palms flat on the earth.
I had never heard a person pray with such reluctance.
>He was afraid of what he prayed to.
He splashed water over the rocks. Is it true
>that if we have no objections, we have no self?

6

Berry-time before the first rains: the dogwood's umbel
like pale blue persimmons, grapes of mountain holly.
Hard-nippled and frost-blue, the juniper berries we stumble

across might be poison. They might, we think, crawling,
lost in the deep woods. *Lost in the woods?*
We amuse ourselves in expatriate voices. A baby is crying

but the sprig of snowberry we hang over the crib is said
to ward off ghosts. We sleep, then find
night hooves between the raspberries. Before us, the birds

dive-bomb the chokecherry, crass and clumsy on its wine.
We live as if in a foreign land, the soil consecrated
to spirits we don't know, who do not know us. We are blind,

yet a brilliance flies through us, angled, belated,
last of the butterfly days. The yellow glue from their bindings
dries and breaks. Wings fall from each other, unweighted.

Which world do insects fall through, ours or theirs, confiding
a life too precious, too astute? A haze
drifts over our minds, blue-green the filaments. Their tidings

have to hit fast—two minutes or less—the ad agencies say.
Is the mystic world the one we *don't* inhabit?
The dark soil of each season is indicative of the veils

we kick through, the wool-gray needle-flecked, the lambent
green. Each crossing stone is marked
by bird or bear. We are hierophants who don't care, a gambit

that gives us pause for our exhaustion. We have embarked
in this country, our expectations dim, a ceiling
of hieroglyphs over us—unread, no longer remarked upon.

The Big Dipper we recognize. It seems to be reeling,
perhaps from the fumes and the height. Yet, there is a channel
opening, though it comes without name. It is kneeling

toward us like the blue—prescient of damage, a mantle
studded with violet thistle and the wild thorn.
The rains begin, signaling a return to an interior we straddle

between the office and the forest. We celebrate, mourn
the fact that, as the critics say, contemporary life *is* urban life.
We dress in shades of eggplant, Asian pears, and corn,

though often we pick up radio signals in our dreams at night.
Our children merge with their heroes
from video games. They fling the furniture, wield the knife.

But who will we go to to exorcise them? If we can close
our eyes, the shade of trees will find a home in us,
brown butterflies of the fallen cones. If we could disclose

our goodness—it was Emerson who said the universe
is an externization of the soul. I return
to the waterfall and my return carves a path, the numinous

act of going forward, toward what I love: maidenhair fern,
the dark, herb-soft stain the waters rise to.
What can you walk blindfolded to? What have you learned

by heart? The feldspar and mica boulders create anew
a voice able to bear the weight of centuries.
With sleek resolve, it hides in wave-pitch, under rubble, spew

of harmonics and stone. But what is *it*? What is the allure
for us in the rush of wind and water, that we always
think we hear more? It doesn't contain the finger of Saint Peter,

a bit of the Tree Cross, or the red scab torn from the days
of Saint Francis, not reliquaries we have crated
to museums from Assisi, or myrrh inside its alabaster blaze.

Here: words that won't bore the gods with pleading, our sated
and beggarly attempts at humility. Here are words
that have drowned in the creek in our stumbling and freighted

passion to cross it. We have tried to name without knowledge
of the Native names for willow, initiates, confused
without an order or invitation. We listen to how the water herds,

then, hugging its depths, how the dark opens the bruised
flanks of her thighs. And we who are restless
watch the autumn come, employing the air with its yellow ruse.

7

I, who bleed, in a trance of salts
watch my mukluks make a trough in the snow
                toward noon which is dark enough for electric lights
                toward winds that arrive, gray disturbances
The instruments of the waterfall come forward and retreat
I don't glance to the left, as if I know
                that my offering will remain where I have left it
                pulp of the chokecherries I packed up the hill
after jelly-making, a crimson turbulence
North, on the reservation the winter rituals are held
                in the trailer, in the sweat lodge, inside the ill
                I hum a song for the bear
one the old man taught me, for the dark mound I saw in the flatbed
of a pickup parked at Walmart, scraped of all but its residual fur
                I lean and lean against the thorn
                of our north wind
The silver shield which lines the earth
pulls at my hem—collapse of the raspberry vine
                its tawny leaves hung, collapse of the tuft of gilt-brown
                ryegrass which opens like a calyx over my boots
Though I am unable to tell how long
one must climb to reach the howling, or where coyote tracks might
                crosshatch the higher field, I sign
in a language I don't know how to speak
                What answers me assumes that I am fluent
Insurgent, the water slides in a thin layer under ice
                It is black dogged and worried through the rock
Would it trade me such open eyes, the subversive gravity of its voice

8

The giveaway dance

May your nephew from Fort Peck be healed from the leukemia
May your sister find her courage and drop her crackhead boyfriend
May Sam get a kidney he goes three times a week for dialysis
May your grandson who has started to have seizures from the Ritalin
May the young man who was stabbed—a good ranch hand they say
May my aunt with diabetes give up her Carlo Rossi
May my uncle survive his heart attack he is only thirty-seven
May the nurses have pity on him and treat him well
And if he does go—because we don't want to challenge the illness—
May his spirit find his people and not linger
Here where it is harsh may the slumlord fix the plumbing
Here what the young ones have left for the cities
May those three old men the healers who now stand for the people—
  see how they struggle to stand up—
Here is a jar of wild chokecherry jam
Here is a pouch of Old Red Man Lucky Strike
Here is a dollar bill for each of your fifteen grandchildren
  see how they dance with empty hands
Here is the fish tank the rest of the bannock
  toilet paper army jacket a Pendleton blanket
Here in the old days grandpa gave away the car and the furniture
  and finally he gave away the house
Here in the trailer house on the reservation
Here where the ragged last of the tribe come with ribbons
Here where the medicine man hangs them in the bundle
  and sets the bundle swinging with a stick
Now since the black spades of aspen have hit the ground
Now because the drumbeat has not changed and has not stopped
We hold the gifts behind our backs and the snow field darkens
May the wind scour the treeless plastic caught in fences
May the man who walks the blizzard not be an apparition
May twenty below on the high line may the loud crunch of tires
May your mother at the cemetery her white cross made of plywood
May the lit cigarette help us to go back

There where the berry soup the rendered lard and raw kidney
There where the tripe apples cookies and white bread
There where the coffee on early and the water for tea
May those watching us may the old men not forget to name them
May the tree people the rock people the kingfisher the eagle
May the dead who are just one threshold between us may their fugitive
voices

find us

9

A Madonna sits in a painting in the Castelvecchio in Verona,
a tapestry deep with scarlet and gold hung behind her.
It is meant to be a garden, but without Renaissance
perspective, the blue-winged angels seem to eat from her hands.
Joggers cross the medieval bridges over the Adige.
Six o'clock traffic stalled by the Roman arena, now the opera.
Time is everywhere / unmoving / in the evenings of the world.

I wake at four a.m. in an ancient room in the Hotel Scalzi,
one with twenty-foot ceilings and bare walls. There is a window
over the alley which I kept open even as I slept. Students
drinking wine below. Time is a cloud above me, dissolving into
faces, voices, sinking and rising the *duomo, palazzo,*
and under them, as part of the apse, the stonework of paleo-
Christian basilicas, and under that, the temples and the baths.

There's nothing interesting on this path, the Cree boy says
back in Montana. The dogwood buds are turning red,
leaf of strawberry. The land is soft again, after rain, as we step
on moss and lichen. But where is his ancestry in this?
The loggers have painted blue streaks on the trees to be saved.
There is honey, what the boy calls the tree's sap.
He has never learned the language his great-grandfather speaks—

What if a bear came, he jokes. What if great-grandma did?
If there are thresholds on this earth beyond our ability
to apprehend them, *the quality of the affection—in the end—*
that has carved the trace, the marble threshold of the cathedral
worn halfway down by the pious, this footpath, the evening
sweat rocks, the name for bear—evening, we like to call it,
an evening of the glare of day, a force somehow opposite to gravity.

No water falling.
No water to cross over the damp sand
between rocks.
Moss on the rocks still green yet.
After that, the jam scorched.
Guests came with lice in their thick braids.
The motorcycle was stolen from the backyard.
A young rodeo rider
who got drunk at the bar
forgot his horse
was still tied to his trailer.
Seventy miles an hour down the freeway
that night.
After that, the fires began in earnest.
We hear that firefighters stumble
into abandoned mines
that have since become the refuge of snakes.
Yellow. Dark. The winds pick up.
Can any of us run fast enough?
Squirrels, rabbits, the porcupines die.
A black bear leaves paw prints on the front door.
Large toad on the road which we run over.
By now the woods are closed to us.
We have packed and left twice,
each time taking different things with us.
We hear the deer
as we try to sleep in the heat, their small cries,
the scuff of their hooves.
If we leave the door open: webs, dust, hair,
the dead bodies of grasshoppers and flies.
We used to be full of the beauty of the world,
to be full like that the accomplishment.
Now, the smoke and heat deafen us.
No water falling.
No stars on the gray limbs of willow, alder.

Instead, green bleeding down into the industrial parks, strewn
with the remnants of teenage luck: used condoms, contraband
beer, with the useless prohibitive next to the cement plant. There
is a water line drawn on the land. We often cross it, run into it, a
sluice through the salt ditch and blue yarrow.

The miners swarm like ants, dirty, hungry, having left their
homes and families in the east. It is not food or shelter they are
after—you've heard they feed dead cattle and poultry bedding
to their cows—but the commodities, the art and furniture, the
peccadilloes: lava lamps, infinity pools, pink flamingos.

There is a certain emptiness between the ancient years of roaming
and the end of roaming, the old song and dance gone, the gods
waiting for their complements. How huge this country is and
how we've filled it. The woman in the desert subdivision leads
workshops in correct listening, although it would be a different
place here, blue dragonfly, dry species, without the Roman
columns, without the irrigation.

Whether or not we are part of this, should we still feed their
angels, we who love our quick summers of breath? Fog by the
wayside, freckled and blue. If we forget the new series, the
undercoat of lupine, and have to piece it anew day by day? If profit
isn't involved, should we be interested?

. . . .

_____

. . . .

_____

Obviously,
we are bent over in the dark, rocks gloved with the earth's heat.
Spirits buzzing. And the water pails clanging. Coterminous
      with three blue grouse
who heave themselves up from their cotes, launch their frightened
          bodies through the air.

The first answers
are often surface ones. Though death has a feel to it, we are
home here with leaf and dark trunk. *Leaf*
      shaped like teardrop, heart, scallop, wing,
tongue, arrow, flesh, feathers, star. Unlike the needles
         which form a curtain here.

No answers,
only the names of things, burdock and rue, the creek bottom gulch
draw darkening. We're not to pray after dark, if you believe what
      you're told, and you do.
Oh, grandfather, you're almost blind but it's not late,
         only the shadows gathering in afternoon.

See the lights there, below us, past the trees—sheer water, all shine

III

The Directions

1 Creator

Some farther shining behind the far shining of the sun
lit by a billion stars which one is god
This small provinciality   this treetop of desire
and those below us sphere upon sphere
There is too much going on for us to keep up with
Owls and mice with their eyes open in the dark
We pray to the things we love the broken bird tree rock
yet word comes in of trouble from the outer place
There are those who will always leave before their time
the summer   my brother   the turquoise flies
We are separated by distance   too many mirrors
Dirt swirls in the dirt road after the rains
Every day we wait for opportunity and hear nothing
For instance everyone we know we think is crazy
A. piles her belongings in the center of a room for a year
B. walks the perimeters   testing the life of branches
We call god deaf and dumb
We call vegetation *it* because we don't know its gender
We serve raspberries and the room fills with their perfume
It is difficult to imagine beyond anything
but I'm sure that's where it's found   the broad sweep
we are constantly translating   Lord to
spirit   one god to this in all her or is it his emanations

2 Soul

There is something all right in giving yourself halfway
if you understand the danger, the hugeness of the thing,
that you're not up for it. All night the moon shines,
showing you how trees breathe. Pines become the thing
they are that you forget, those with whom you live your life.
You could go out into the world or in and leave the thing,
which is like a bridge, clear for the others.
Twice in the backyard, a flash of yellow in the willows,
once getting wood, once calling out your door. What thing
was its south, its side of shadow? Everything—
seasons, direction, elements, the moon—divides itself
into colors and gestures, into secondary lodgings
of the half-breed or the deciduous though some things
are blind: blind soul of thunder, blind soul of feathers
on its back. The dark clouds are ominous, bringing things
that you need. Yet the mind continues to cast out
like a prison beacon for suspects, to pounce on something
it barely sees. You want instead to be chosen, gifted,
touch your hands on the earth to remember and remember.
The sky is silver from last night's rain in the low spots
below the mountain. The sky is not one thing
but many highs and lows. As a child, it hurt you when things
were ugly—a bar, an alley, a tar roof to sunbathe on,
all of it so tired and unhappy, certainly never happy
to see you. The green world then became
your happiness, those with quiet voices and four souls.

3 The Ceremonial

Moonbeam coreopsis next to green beans in the garden,
cosmos, Icelandic poppies, bachelor buttons of all hues—
constant growth that makes me feel that I am shrinking.
One should, I have heard, make oneself pleasing to the gods,
fragrant with acts of kindness, the smoke of ritual,
although one should stand for one's people before anything,
promises made to dead ones, selfish concerns,
that the meat was pale and watery and I had hated killing it,
that the moon was in the lake and grew leaves as it grew later,
that I have decided I do not like houseguests.
What I do like is to draw a long distance in the heat, one side
white, embossed, one blue with strawberries.
I like to wear my own leaf, striated like the chokecherry,
wear it over my heart so that I am recognized.

4 The Old Ones

Black clusters hang from the chokecherry bush
which fills now with the heaviness of robins.
The robins honk and cluck
as they strong-arm the cherries from their stems.
Down here, we are fat with emotion.
Down here, the singular cry of each hawk as it hunts
midair is a sound lighter than the dark around it.
The loud ones will always steal the morning,
but the goldfinch is the prize, the one who dazzles.
Here by the window, I try not to startle them.
I know that there are many more trees than mine.
I often ask them questions before I go to sleep.
I am done with the priests and can relax now.
The natives say the sound of wind through
needles of pine is the voice of the old ones talking—
old as in those who were in the world before us.
The larger animals woof from the edge of the woods.
The mountain maple leaves are brittle.
If I forget to face north or address them by name,
will the year proceed like a failed experiment?
We have always lived with the dead. Why without them?

5 Animals

Some, plump and green, flies buzzing over them.
Then silver, light so they lift from the dirt road.

Some with deep eyes, the grace of exchange,
seem too tame, like women and could be killed for it.

The larger move soundlessly through a forest
that would betray them. With the loon,
they own the mad songs and are undone by them.

Some, like a blessing, quick and light with seven
tongues, in winter sing the summer to appease us.

Some are treasures worth nothing, like fool's gold
in a stream. They come with waxed wings,
depart in a day, pull the faded wool across our eyes.

But what yours? *Yours?* Something that speaks
only to you? Shiny pelt you saw grousing under logs?

They birth, half-asleep, ounces of themselves,
nursing their young in the dark. Some we never see,

or only in disguise. They gather in choruses,
like the fates who read the hillsides and haunt the stars.

Those who are black spirit, close to the water birch
and spruce shadow, those who exist only
in abstraction—how is it we think we know them better?

6 Shooting Star

Swamp cold. Metallic. Air,
          as I run past the creek,
rises into stars. The creek is lowered but continues.
"What to believe,"
we keep asking point-blank, as if we
          couldn't find it in the order of our work,
the lights that connect, quick and bristling
through the leaves. One works,
          does one not, for the experience?
Yet everyone gambles: a week without the pills,
          without a job, watching for signs of plummet.
To go one way, like Socrates, until a voice says stop,
          so, prophecy as locked gate, as edge?
My brother, the day after his suicide attempt,
          calls on his cell phone from a deli.
Wanting to die, he still has to eat
and eat alone, chicken mass-produced and fried for him.
Death is what we have
          when we look up at the stars.
It stretches into a long thing, no quick matter.
          Though we are often unsure
whether death woos us or not:
          our punishment for distraction is distraction.

7 The Poles

To not have to choose   between one or the other
To be deciduous and needled   and let the needles fall
Grasses   the black-tipped and light-tipped
To light the flame of god   burrow into the secret cave
Gods born with ambiguous genitalia
We pass reefs that cap the waves of yellow foothills
Underneath hide amphitheaters   pictographs of deer
Musk ox skulls left on the hewn altars
Suffering the chalice to hold wine   and the divine
Manipulative   punishing   complicating the other
Appealed to only by following   webs and rituals
Messy   mad in a way   a swarm of talk spirits
Gambling   gamble what we know   try to get a good meal
Or sex in between   at least pray the truck is fixed for good
This one's about duality   right now they are at war again
Outdoors is dark with the lights on   but without
A mild unnamable color   four deer eating the garden rot

8 Light

An artist places the intangible
            and tangible objects on the table together:
drift of diamond light from the Sky of the Mind
with the Asian poppy, the plate of wild seedling plums.

The direction is set, sun caught in eastern branches
when our empty hands have their other side of fullness.
            Still life: morning star. Moon.
Dawn. The sun (who is *A Bird Singing in the Moonlight*).

What to believe? Even the question fades,
            dissipates in preparation for its answer, glad
to be in the present which is dark and slow and dull.
Glad at last to lie on the ground. To sleep. To drink water.

And the observance of solitude. Day by day, they say,
            and the use of herbs, the reordering of the body.
Tell the people to help each other, they say
from the other side. Things are only the crosshatch of actions.

Still life: morning star. One begins again.
            One begins and hopes to avoid getting lost again.
Still life. How many children know
the stations of the moon, the *b* for birth and *d* for destruction?

The sun moves through a chorus of wastelands.
            The sun rises and rises. Still, this arrangement.
Winter bouquet. (Rose Haws and
Hellebore.) Each one a harbinger. Each shadowing the other.

9 Rock

Clear away a spot, gooseberry or its equivalent—
turn around and face yourself down, the skeletal
pebbles. "Meanwhile" we begin, one foot already
in the story We Grow to Love Where We End Up,
the story of the autochthonic. Who has been here
the longest? Who knows the songs to sing,
what direction to turn and when? In the beginning,
the rocks remained unnamed, say the Cree.
They had to ask for their tasks. We take our families
for granted, here, on the other side of winter,
when we are raw, in emotional rags.
How crooked, how irrational are tree branches.
Do the rocks leap, have they survived their decisions,
sullage of the granite, skull after the cancer—
Grandfather Rock, the Cree say, spirit of conundrum:
I will stand   I will stand for you   I will stand up for you.

10 Earth

To pull at any piece would be to risk such unraveling:
femur, hip bone, fibula, wrists bound together with cloth.

The eye moves, stops at two legs made of straw
and mud, one long foot, the glyph of a bandaged head.

The eye approaches word by word now: slope of the human
shoulder, fingers, their span. How is it we didn't see them

before? The dead are deflated, strung with roots of grass.
The earth twists its fabric through the mass grave—

on average, seven bodies per square inch. Surprising,
this hellishness, though we have been warned in Bosch,

in Dante, but to see them, caught in their transformations?
A shoe sole, for instance, its familiar figure eight—we know

instinctively that this is ours. Earth, the grief place.
Odd, she is so alone. Yet she hears even my light footsteps.

Culpable, elastic, she takes my weight. Can she absorb our
failures? Can we be part of the response, a *second nature*,

as you will? Mother of all things, we fester here. The pine sap
hardens to blue. So much violence under the blossom.

11 Fire

The centuries have a way of being male.
WALLACE STEVENS

White velocity. We dare not interrupt you.
                         Stream of light in the light.
Gender. The supreme fiction? Gender.
             The alchemy? Stars you build and stamp out.
What is old: you are sweeping through it,
             jumping the creek. Arnica. Cedar waxwings.
The pale pink spider.   Your ash, already, anointing them.
             I cut the tree that fell in this winter's wind.
I rake twigs into piles and pull the runners from the tines
             to hand to you, to use for your quick ceremonies.
Can you take what is negative, correct our mistake? We have
             such plans for amelioration. *As below, so above.*
Lightning. Sun. *As above, so below.* Igneous, metamorphic.
You are the weed that grows spiky and voluptuous.
You are the verb, sprung from the seven sprouts of morning
                         to the twenty-two of afternoon.
             Fire beneath our lids, the farce of you.

12 Herbs

Iris-weather, rain of
grasses, pines, sages: green sensorium of the world.

Here, for instance, awake
on the other side of midsummer, I note what has been,
            what needs to. I mean the complete

sensorium, including the dream, smoothness of this table,
            for instance, which I painted sea-green,

Persephone caught
staring at a flower. Can beauty be compensation for grief?
            Our own heliotaxis.

Like the robin, for instance, at sunset, atop the high spruce,
            turning its breast to the sun,
or the layering through our lives of a particular herbage,

sweet pine, the prairie sages, the pink-rooted grass—
            the American grass we braid and burn.

Even without belief, we must admit
to a certain sense of holiness, in their green-lit transparence,

in their capacity for light, and how our eyes are drawn to it.
Metaphysical.
            To be changed internally from afar.

And to consecrate? I make my requests
near the creek, holding a leaf, in the stony soil of the near-field.

IV

*Radiant opacity. Speaking earth. Weren't we
thick once as birds and awake together?*
Forrest Gander

Demeter

1

I grind the nut-hard pellets, flowers of the grasses—
wheat, kamut, rye, spelt, corn—add honey
the bees have gathered from the white clover
and red clover, the compressed buds of the yeast
cake, oil from safflower. I understand
how the inner life can disappear from neglect,
why the painters are so enamored of the surface.
Light today dramatic, almost too intense a green,
light superinduced, as the ancients say, on earth.
I stray outdoors, bring buckets to the raspberries,
work according to the earth's axis,
east for the sweet peas, west for summer squash,
in the end, what we must mean by the metaphysical.
Yes, she is a spirit, clear-browed and beautiful.
Yes, she is a dark one full of light.
I deadhead the irises, water the smaller clumps
of violet, find the transplants buried under the more
established. We all have our secrets, public
and private. We all have our symbols, our initiations.
I remember the comments from my teachers
as a child. I spoke so quietly they couldn't hear me.
I thought that to speak up meant to speak against.
Later, I learned that each of us is responsible
for her own story. Mine, that I love flowers
more than people. The ancients believe we come
back as plants—a row of white columbine,
a field of blue flax—unindividuated, cyclic and hence,
godlike. What *determines* these questions of matter?
Earth, the monstrosity of its soil?
Yet earth is where we learn to recognize each other.

2

It is her spirit that keeps her from rotting,
from the body collapsing in so much heat.
I offer her the bowl with ice cubes,
burn dry grass, cedar, fill the air with bee balm.
If it were me, I would say that touch hurts.
But she is wordless like her kind and allows me.
I grow toward death, too, even perhaps
a violent one, too sudden or too late.
What vastness. Yet I worry about her body
put into the ground, rain soaking her clothes,
the ants she will displace. *It doesn't matter*
people will say about anything—though we
are matter. We are here in this realm.
Her father has obstinately gone off his pills.
Her sister eats only lunch meat and white wine.
And her brother? He cuts his wrists only deep
enough to make them bleed. All are candidates
and all, of course, will die. But who next?
And how? With softness, with grace, at twilight,
that deeper death-blue? The gods
have closed the road before me. Perhaps
they know that I would follow her, tossed off
the summit to the rocks. Yet it is when
I hear her rise now from her bed that I am afraid.

3

The ruffled red skirts of the poppies
strangle the crop of green beans
because I could not bear to weed them.
Dark pink, the depth of sunflower—
all more, all satiate with light. And here,
in the middle, the illness of my friend
who died just as spring sun hit the porch,
who smelled the first rains but missed
the grasshoppers. After her death,
the tidal swell of summer and its events,
a concert of waltzes, arugula and dates,
nocturnes of orchids and blues,
and a play one evening in a village without
a name, squash blossoms stuffed
with nectarine. Now war, which we forgot,
not having ever lived through one, discord
with our families, too much food left on
the shelves until we are simply bored with it.
While the garden, open-faced to the coming
frost, raspberries crumbling at a touch,
continues to offer its daily sixteen beans,
poppy seeds white as the roe of trout.
The larvae inside the hornet's nest pressed
to my pane pulse toward stingers to be fed.
And the finite ones, a dragonfly, downed
by one paw, azure as the mountain bluebird
now leaving—there will be no more planting.
Sky darkens with rain. The ornament
of image seems false, though here is a stone
rimmed by late red and blue flax,
and I have laid cornflowers upon it. No truth,
but the heart aches for what it could not
tend to before, for the words said in summer
we cannot take back, for those identified
by their flowers amid the straw.

Sleep Comes from the Flowers

Three hours the deer sleep, then back to the vowels
of the water, the all-day drowse of mice and grass and owls.
Snow like white dahlias. Deer curled together like buds.
The ice in the creek cannot bear any more cold
and cracks each night into a thousand mums. Petal
of the squirrel's lid, closed and safe. The trees stay awake,
or asleep, as you prefer. Like me, they take
what is offered them. But the animals strive, pace the fields
for food or mates. Do moths sleep together or apart?
Everything with consciousness must sleep, not merely rest,
though bird dreams last nine seconds or less
and fish can sleep while swimming. What part of the body
continues? The twin butterflies inside my chest
spin and spin from their cocoons. The heart like a loon
cries out in its dream and still manages to stay afloat.
We are summoned to sleep like a vocation,
perhaps a religious one, some drop from activity into loam.
The dark blooms in winter on the walls of the canyon.
We achieve our imagination in increments.

Calypso

Sister leaf   here where the bronze bark the silver
the meadow a flat place and elk have torn the thickets
here where the fairy movement of light
A place of vast particulars   butterflies   tragedies
How would anyone know looking at it from the moon

The soul is heavy   it belongs to earth not air
where the lower rank of gods live swarming
I pass by them until I am under their spell   the flies
and ants and orchids   I who am willing to entertain

What does the sense of privacy in flowers consist of
lanceolate   pink lip   the spotted lobes
What is drawn to me proleptic   the petals are fading
on the threshold in the haunt in my private enchantments

Birds on the other hand hide from my gaze in the leaves
Do I do well   look well   do they like me for it
The creek is high   my home flowers
in the range of purples   *sister tenants of the middle deep*

The men of course are leaving but I stay on the island
where water slosh   where the scent of lily
In medias res   there is loss of course but look what
is to be gained   one steps into a softer boundless world

Calypso   my name means to cover   to bury   lips
closed to the rain   even I know the temptation to forget
Isn't everything right here   on the surface
moss and gentian   why go further risk the same mistakes
if I can't see   if I don't know that I am beautiful

The Ice-Lit Upper World

title from a line in a poem by George Oppen

The tree emits a sound like a tiny silver bell.
The tree fills with cedar waxwings.
The tree is lightning struck, the birds just silhouette.
The tree bends in the most improbable windsong.
Like summer again, the fires burning inside the houses.
I paint out the yellow bloom of sage against the snow.
Despite my maturity, there is something girl-like,
they say, too innocent about me, which means
I am not interested in having sex with them.
High in these mountains the skies have a sheen.
Clouds pass as if skating on ice.
I am content to transform them into a handful of inner life.
I move slow because of the red wine.
My father who has the devil in him has tried everything
to get him out. I write him letters
and decide not to touch: wet underslope of the boulder,
dry foreskin of a leaf that fits my thumb.
Although I am not particularly good, animals trust me,
birds show me their wings.
To step into the world I found a word: viridescence.
It means to be illuminated, green.
All night, the brown and speckled hawks fly above my sleep.
There is only one small unhappiness to do with love.

River Reeds

You called me back to the bridge, before we reached the house,
before spring, pre-spring. The creek was rushing.
We had just run through drifts. We'd been knee-deep in snow.
You could hardly catch your breath for all your smoking—
three packs a day now since you've been writing on Rimbaud.
We spoke of Eros. I had just read *The Golden Ass*,
first mention in our literature of Psyche. Together, we recited
her trials and how she solved them: the sheep's wool, pile
of seeds, vial of water. We, who are failing miserably at them all.
You said you told your new lover how long we had been friends,
about the jealousy this friendship has always caused.
She looked at you sideways, *Do you love her*?
And that is why I love you, because you laughed and said *of course*.
I was sure this meant we were out of danger. Sun, early April.
We did not hold hands. Not lovers, not siblings, not companions.
Then what? It was the river reeds who told Psyche
to gather tufts off the twigs while the dangerous sheep were sleeping.
It was the ants who helped her sort her piles of seeds.
I said I think about love differently now, with disillusion after pain.
You said disillusion is part of the dialectic of wisdom.
You are young. You don't know how death sneaks up on one.
Will you give me two sops of bread to feed the dogs in hell?
We stood on the bridge before we walked back toward my house,
where my lover would serve you red wine and grilled salmon.
And love's trials? Remember that I showed you
the secret frozen pool. Remember the barley, the flax seed and fennel.

Orpheus

When you left, I stepped off the edge
of my goodness onto a rickety bridge.
Myself in pain at what I have done
is not the same as the pain without you.

All of the unattached, the phonemes,
the chickadees unfed, half the spades
of sorrow—just live, the under-gods
say, but the body rebels at its silencing.

There is a cache of garbage in the forest,
the pitiful remains of a bad week.
Only the chance I might make something
beautiful, though I am torn apart by dogs.

I find you everywhere: snowberries
on such thin stems they float in air,
scattering of cigarette butts on the porch.
I believed I could only be killed once.

For years, love was my subject,
fragrance of wood at the moment it splits,
weight of it in my arms. Not yours
to piece excuses into an understanding.

In the barn-light of half-sleep, beyond
the circle of who I am, cold reaches into
corners of shoes, my pumpkin
house, ochre-lined pit of wildflowers.

I live in a country gone mad, in a world of
public beheadings. I sing my grief to all
who breathe, the ancient drama where
I get to play a role, one you cut out for me.

Sibyl

Begin simply, with advice, strange speech
on the edge of our reason, snail path over the waves.
Through the pinhole of silence it all falls through.
Through the lie escaping someone's lips.
You are a cry from a well, not words on the wind.
You are mumblings from a cave, half-decipherable.
Where *are* you? The half-human voice
we hear in the creek is, in the end, image, not cadence.
Spill of the valuable on the banks.
We realize the impossible bargain we want,
access and return, not this cramming of syllables.
A trysting place that never changes location.
A bright feathered aviary with only one bird singing.
Tightrope above the increasing fields of pain.
Look, we've bought a lot of things wholesale,
including the idea of a voice, thinking you would then
belong to us. We have knelt before the altar,
love-poor with pine boughs, held the photocopies
of our childhoods to the flames.
They were almost inflammable, sleeveless, green.
In them, it was evident you were retreating.
We come to you in our dissension, caught in limbs.
We come to you with our war paint on.
If the method is retrieval, birth from clay and sperm,
sunlight the burning of past fuel, perhaps
that is the problem. We exiled you from the world,
banished you to the bleeding-hut of introspection.

Debt

He asked us to repay a cock to Asclepius
after discoursing on the nature of the other world,
the upper earth which is heaven
and this sediment he was leaving us,
we who live in the hollows,
this cock pit, this barnyard, this purse from a sow's ears,
full of bills, coins, brine, *this endless slough of mud.*
How charging
was his tale of the earth seen from above, the multicolored
ether ball glowing.
Faced with his death, Socrates sent his wife home—
no woman to light candles, perhaps rub the skin with oil—
while we watched clouds lift from the window.
Could we live there, too,
without the willow, dirt, sound of water,
without yoke of custom, what he called our shaggy hearts?
When he lay down, when his legs were heavy,
when he dreamt of the colored ball and told us of it,
he said love is a conversation in time.
Even so, we had stopped talking, afraid of misunderstanding.
We wished we could understand it as he did.

The Under World

We have come this far because where we were, things
were no longer possible.
RENÉ CHAR

1

I had an idea midwinter. It was ruby, glistening. It was garnet,
menstrual. I would have it on my table, centered, a red rocking
thing to measure time. Which doesn't move, they say, which is
an illusion. Unemployed: traveling to the woodpile and coming
back with sticks. I know the shrunken world is an experiment.
Bird shell caught in the teeth. So far I have waited mole-eyed, the
body puffy. What huge desperation devises these tests? I open
my eyes when I have been asked to keep them closed. I peek and
then the fascists come down on me. I have tried to be a good
therapeutic model, to choose to be happy, that jingling of coins.
But there is no room for heart in the cold earth place.

2

The world circles around me with its pack of lies. Shall I give it one last chance? And another? Over there with its arms hotel and dealers, over there with its expensive slip removed? I walk the seven miles and the trees, the creek—all with their hands tied, forbidden to speak to me. Only the birds are alive, who pester me with the ridiculous: *What happened to your work? Who stole it from you? What will you have to do to get it back?* One lives the life one was meant to, or one doesn't. I set out my offerings, violet and puce, my tinted vials of flower remedies. Beware. There are dangers to surpass, tricks to outguess, especially the straw names of those who love you.

3

Something tells me it was left in the roots of a tree. *You do have your magic but it is not in things.* Can I put it in things? I have the turtle shell bleached in the sun. I have all the tiny replicas. *Perhaps this is the story you have been telling yourself too long, the just-born waddling to the sea: I am not weak. I am not fragile. I am just not ready.* The child so wants to believe she will do anything to keep the beautiful voices talking. The myth that we can go back again. The myth of the natural conclusion. Which is in ruins back there, salt drifting between the pillars of the city we abandoned to art. Resist. When we first drew the stars into their constellations, all the unconstellated were lost.

4

What possible fingers at the edges stitching? Provisional. A regional if not
a global warming. A sense that something is in store for us. Midnight, a
water dipper begins to sing, careless lifting of the heart. As if we might
explain things to each other. *Soon. Monsoon.* Water opens itself to itself,
elk tracks fill with thaw. Nevertheless, this season, though similar, is
far different than the rest. An arc I can inscribe with a bandaged hand.
Must each love be an abandonment of another? Where swallows lived:
pockmarks on the cliff face. Where paintings hung now light-housed
by darker walls. To begin to see the goodness that comes out of loss
demands a certain generosity. *Soon,* not the but and yet of stall.

5

I had the empty center. They watched me go down it. I had the hole to fill.
With oilspill, with mother-soaked rags. The daughter said mine and tried
to filch it. They should not think I am unhappy here. Look at my pantry:
four eggs, a cloak of milk. Here, at last, I am The Only One. There, I was
responsible—for nights cast in pear-light, the noon with saffron. Hillsides
of the herbals in sequin. I could not sustain it and things went bad
again. The emerald circling my wrists no longer binds me to that forest.
My names are often far from me and I do not answer them. Calm, not
dead. Snug, not toppling on my high-heel nerves. Here, love no longer
flypapers words so they stick. Here, love has been scraped from the vat.

6

Daughter, the cadence of daughter, lost in the rhythm of wishing back. I
wanted to be a flower, not a monster. Delicate, shaded. I didn't want to be
an urchin, grabbing at cake, resentful of any too-small kindness. Behind
the daughter is a mother who is a daughter who is a mother. We talk
out of both sides of our mouths. One side silent, the other propending.
Is that when the *day* dreaming began? There was light in the entering,
a chemical imbalance, more light than I had been exposed to since
childhood. Where I could shine in my own spit. Where I could trumpet
my own sphere. Where I could rend my raw tent into the vastness.

7

Up in the air. A peculiar phrase. What does it mean that nothing's landed? Rain cloud—hydrangea—its blue hand over the sun. Cloud-god. Rinse me of this winter shame. I have been in the ditch, a blindfold, and thought I was on a train. I have tried to swipe intimacy against the will. Only wood chips in the woodshed, my emptied wagers. It will take time, they say, to wrestle back what's the use from the river you have drowned in. It will take time for the stories to emerge. Seed by seed, the working up through the soil. But is time really accomplished without us? The dark bud unclasping? The stirring of air? The sex-cluck of the robins at the butter dish?

8

Venture: red bud of the new leaf. The private language gone public, a
shelter belt I fashioned, rough-skinned, cooled by pulp. Glove of the
interior, tight-fitting. Sustain this without fear? Shouldn't I cling to the
stalk? Don't I owe them something, those I left behind? Old love: an
oxymoron. Love is the hinge that turns us into opposite wings. Unhinged
into patterns of amplitude. *Half-gathered, when I dropped my bouquet.*
Can we chink in the armor, unhood the hooded prisoner? Can we
really forgive each trespass against us? Too soon, perhaps, this stab at
expedition. Too soon the whitened grasses, the green blades overtaking.
Too soon, the fragrant city, the muddy rampage.

9

When I broke with the earth, in grief, the animals still gathered. The iris skimmed the pond, turning it to azure. I felt the coolness on my arms. Re-pressed. Implying the property of buoyancy. Re-petition. Implying the king or queen might still say yes. Though the soil still clings to me. Though I drag my bootleg pain. Though I still believe in perpetrator and victim. Deep need, I am bending into you. Pulverized by being. Nothing else will wake me. Bite deep my driving hand. If I am progeny of thorns, I am also mother of a sea of roses. If I am sea, I am anaphora. Casting a calm above the undertow. Speak to me, work, or I will be forever lonely. Help me to remember who I am.

Melissa Kwasny is the author of two previous books of poetry, *The Archival Birds* (Bear Star Press 2000) and *Thistle* (Lost Horse Press, Winner of the Idaho Prize 2006). She is also the editor of *Toward the Open Field: Poets on the Art of Poetry 1800-1950* (Wesleyan University Press 2004). She lives in western Montana.

Photo by Joseph Collins.

More Poetry from Milkweed Editions

To order books or for more information, contact Milkweed at (800) 520-6455 or visit our Web site (www.milkweed.org).

Hallelujah Blackout
ALEX LEMON

Music for Landing Planes By
ÉIREANN LORSUNG

Willow Room, Green Door
DEBORAH KEENAN

Invisible Horses
PATRICIA GOEDICKE

The Phoenix Gone, The Terrace Empty
MARILYN CHIN

Atlas
KATRINA VANDENBERG

Milkweed Editions

Founded in 1979, Milkweed Editions is one of the largest independent, nonprofit literary publishers in the United States. Milkweed publishes with the intention of making a humane impact on society, in the belief that good writing can transform the human heart and spirit.

Join Us

Milkweed depends on the generosity of foundations and individuals like you, in addition to the sales of its books. In an increasingly consolidated and bottom-line-driven publishing world, your support allows us to select and publish books on the basis of their literary quality and the depth of their message. Please visit our Web site (www. milkweed.org) or contact us at (800) 520-6455 to learn more about our donor program.

Milkweed Editions, a nonprofit publisher, gratefully acknowledges sustaining support from Anonymous; Emilie and Henry Buchwald; the Patrick and Aimee Butler Family Foundation; the Dougherty Family Foundation; the Ecolab Foundation; the General Mills Foundation; the Claire Giannini Fund; John and Joanne Gordon; William and Jeanne Grandy; the Jerome Foundation; the Lerner Foundation; the McKnight Foundation; Mid-Continent Engineering; a grant from the Minnesota State Arts Board, through an appropriation by the Minnesota State Legislature, a grant from the National Endowment for the Arts, and private funders; Kelly Morrison and John Willoughby; an award from the National Endowment for the Arts, which believes that a great nation deserves great art; the Navarre Corporation; Ellen and Sheldon Sturgis; Target; the James R. Thorpe Foundation; the Travelers Foundation; Moira and John Turner; Joanne and Phil Von Blon; Kathleen and Bill Wanner; Serene and Christopher Warren; and the W. M. Foundation.

MINNESOTA
STATE ARTS BOARD

NATIONAL
ENDOWMENT
FOR THE ARTS
A great nation
deserves great art.

TARGET.

THE McKNIGHT FOUNDATION

Interior design by Paul Hotvedt
Typeset in Lawrence, Kansas
by Blue Heron Typesetters
Printed on acid-free Rolland paper
by Friesens Corporation